OPEN OUR
hearts

2/1/10

Best wishes for a Holy Lent.

F. Tom Iacoroul.

This booklet for faith groups to use during Lent is a rich treasure that brings together biblical insight, a simple and user-friendly methodology, and practical suggestions for living God's word.

Most Reverend Ricardo Ramirez
Bishop of Las Cruces

Conversion means being called by God's word to put into action what you have heard in a community of friends. This is the simple, enriching path that *Open Our Hearts* provides for you. Here is a Lent to remember!

Paul Philibert, O.P.
Southern Dominican Province

Sr. Donna Ciangio and Fr. Thomas Iwanowski offer a comprehensive tool for serious faith development. *Open Our Hearts* is friendly, self-directing, and solidly rooted in the Lectionary . . . a great resource.

Bill Huebsch
Director of ThePastoralCenter.com

An insightful exploration of the Lenten scriptures and realistic reflections on daily life . . . . A fine resource for Lent!

Zeni Fox, PhD
Professor of Pastoral Theology
Immaculate Conception Seminary, Seton Hall University

OPEN OUR hearts

A Small-Group Guide for an active lent

Cycle C

Donna L. Ciangio, O.P.

Thomas B. Iwanowski

ave maria press AmP notre dame, indiana

Founded in 1865, Ave Maria Press is a ministry of the Indiana Province of Holy Cross.

www.avemariapress.com

ISBN-10 1-59471-242-5   ISBN-13 978-1-59471-242-5

Cover image © Bob Jensen / Alamy

Cover and text design by John R. Carson.

Printed and bound in the United States of America.

Contents

⫸⎮ Welcome

Welcome to *Open Our Hearts*! This booklet was created with you in mind—Catholics who will gather in small groups this Lent to learn from and encourage one another. It is designed to help you open your heart and mind to the Good News of Jesus Christ and to live according to that Good News. The purpose of Lent and of this faith sharing program is not simply to listen, pray, and learn about our faith but to put that faith into action. The purpose of Lent and of your time with your small group is to help change the way you live each day so that your life will more closely reveal to the world the Kingdom of God.

Open Our Hearts invites small group participants to deepen their faith and their service by linking reflection on scripture to their lives as individuals, family members, parishioners, and as Catholics engaged in civil society. Lent is the perfect time for renewal. It is the Church's opportunity to be on retreat—for each of us to take quality time to see where we are with God and how we serve others because of our faith. Each of us is called to deepen our relationship with God every day of our life, and Lent helps us review and recommit ourselves to that relationship and to the good works it calls forth from us.

During Lent, Catholics often gather in small groups to read and reflect on the scriptures. This is a great way to pray and learn and get to know others in a deeper way. The small group process helps us to understand that we are continually invited by God into a loving relationship. It is God who leads us on a journey of faith. As Christians, we are part of a community of believers who need others to support us along the way. The process of sharing our faith involves reflection on the Tradition of the Church as we experience it in our scriptures, doctrines, pastoral initiatives, liturgy, and devotions. This Tradition is necessarily set alongside current events and issues being explored in both the religious and civic arenas. By reflecting with others, we affirm what we believe and how we live out our faith, which should lead us to actions that improve our world in some way.

Faith sharing is a form of prayer when we witness how God is working in each group member. Small groups are also a great way to connect people with each other and invite them into parish ministry and outreach. We hope you find this a great benefit to you in your faith development. May you use this Lent to assess your relationship with God, realign your priorities, and go forth to do good works!

⊰ Using This Booklet

This Lenten booklet is designed for small group reflection and personal prayer in conjunction with the Mass readings for Lent. Groups of this kind do well with about six to eight participants. **Part I** contains outlines for six weekly gatherings that will likely last about ninety minutes each. The weekly reflection anticipates the coming Sunday to help group members prepare for hearing the Word of God proclaimed during the celebration of the Eucharist. Week One is therefore intended to be used during the week of Ash Wednesday, in anticipation of the First Sunday of Lent. Consequently, the last session, Week Six, is rooted in the scripture readings for Palm/Passion Sunday. Following this schedule means that small groups do not meet during Holy Week and can focus instead on the liturgical celebrations of the great Easter Triduum as the pinnacle of our Church year.

Part II contains a reflection for each weekday of Lent and is designed to provide group participants with a simple tool to help them stay focused between group meetings.

The Small Group Format

Preparing for the Session

Group members should prepare ahead of time for each session by reading and reflecting on the scripture and the material for each week. A bible should be available for reading the scripture passages aloud when the group gathers. A facilitator in each group will help members participate, keep the group focused, and monitor time.

Setting the Environment

This provides some hints for the host and/or facilitator on preparing a welcoming place for the group to meet, including creating a simple focal point for prayer and reflection.

Gathering Prayer

The Gathering Prayer centers the group and calls for God's blessing on the group's sharing.

Connecting with Life

This section serves as a guide to the theme of the scripture for the coming Sunday. A few questions help the group move into the reflection each week.

Listening to the Word

A member of the group (preferably with some preparation) reads aloud the Sunday Gospel. The first and second readings may also be proclaimed, depending on the group's preference. But, in the interest of time, the group may choose to hear only the Gospel at each session.

Appreciating the Word

Another group member reads aloud the reflection or commentary, which is focused primarily on the Gospel reading. Brief reflections on the other readings are also included in case the group wishes to reflect on these as well.

Reflecting on My Life

The reflection questions focus on the Gospel. Participants share on a personal level, describing how they apply the Gospel to their lives.

Reflecting on My Home

This section is designed to encourage group members to reflect on how the Gospel is lived at home. Families or households are encouraged to reflect on their faith together and consider prayer and action together.

Reflecting on My Parish

The questions in this section encourage group members to consider how their parish community supports, encourages, teaches, and fosters growth in faith. The facilitator can record these responses and submit them to the parish staff and pastoral council to aid in planning.

Affecting My World

Faith reflection should lead to positive change. What will you do as a result of what you said, heard, or learned from the session? Taking a specific action each week will put the meaning and lessons of the scriptural text into practice.

Sending Forth

The Sending Forth concludes the session and sends members forth to live the Gospel during the week. Participants may choose to add particular intercessions or other prayers.

Evaluation

At the end of each session, the facilitator may ask the group to evaluate the experience using the evaluation form available at the back of this booklet. Another form of evaluation may also be used, such as a simple conversation about how the gathering went, possibly using the form provided here as a springboard. The form is also available for free download at avemariapress.com

Participant Guidelines
for Small Group Reflection

Each small faith sharing group has a facilitator. The facilitator creates a welcoming and prayerful atmosphere. If you are meeting in a parishioner's home, the host prepares a comfortable seating area. The facilitator's role is to keep the group on the topic and the conversation moving. He or she also needs to ensure that everyone has the opportunity to participate. Introverts will likely need a few minutes to think before they are ready to speak, while extroverts generally begin speaking more readily. The facilitator may need to draw out some group members and remind others to allow time for fellow participants to talk.

Everyone in the group shares the responsibility for having a great session. The facilitator should help the group evaluate each session so that any needed improvements can be made. It is also a good idea for either the facilitator or another group member to contact those who could not make the meeting to let them know they were missed and encourage them to come the next week.

A Word about Confidentiality

What is said in the group stays in the group! People grow in their depth of sharing as the trust level grows in the group, so each member should show the utmost respect for each member and for God who lives in each person. Each member should understand that your purpose in meeting is to grow in depth of faith and in relationship with God and one another. Respect each other by commitment to the meeting time and by honoring with confidentiality the personal stories and thoughts that are shared in your time together.

Part I:

Weekly
Small Group
Sessions

Week One: Led by the Spirit

READINGS FOR THE FIRST SUNDAY OF LENT:
- Deuteronomy 26:4–10
- Romans 10:8–13
- Luke 4:1–13

Setting the Environment

 On a table in the center of your group, covered with a Lenten (purple) colored cloth, place a crucifix, a bible, and a lighted candle. Begin the session by slowly making the sign of the cross together.

Gathering Prayer

Be with us, O God, as we begin our Lenten journey.
Strengthen us as we walk the way from sin
   to the font of living water
and recommit ourselves to our baptismal promises.
We ask this in the name of Jesus,
who lives and reigns with you in the unity of the Holy Spirit,
one God, forever and ever.
Amen

Connecting with Life

 The facilitator or another member of the group reads aloud the following introduction then introduces the discussion questions that follow it.

Sometimes in life, people place us in situations that make us uncomfortable and they do so for our own good. Parents may register their shy child for summer camp in order to give that child a chance to make some friends. An academic advisor may insist a student take more advanced courses in order to challenge that student to grow intellectually. An employer may require a subordinate to make a presentation before potential clients in order to instill greater self-confidence in that employee.

Sometimes those in authority lead us to do things we would rather not do, to go places we would rather not go, to confront situations we would rather avoid. And they do so for our own good.

- Think of a time when you were required to do something you would have preferred to avoid, and by doing what you were asked, you grew as a person. Describe that time. What was it like?
- Have you ever encouraged someone to go beyond their comfort zone for his or her own good?

Listening to the Word

 Take a quiet moment to pray a prayer such as, "O Lord, be in our minds, in our hearts, and on our lips that we might listen fully to your Word."

A member of the group then reads aloud the Gospel for the First Sunday of Lent, using the bible from the table in the center of the group.

Gospel Reading: Luke 4:1–13

Filled with the Holy Spirit, Jesus returned from the Jordan and was led by the Spirit into the desert for forty days, to be tempted by the devil. He ate nothing during those days, and when they were over he was hungry. The devil said to him, "If you are the Son of God, command this stone to become bread." Jesus answered him, "It is written, 'One does not live by bread alone.'" Then he took him up and showed him all the kingdoms of the world in a single instant. The devil said to him, "I shall give to you all this power and their glory; for it has been handed over to me, and I may give it to whomever I wish. All this will be yours, if you worship me." Jesus said to him in reply, "It is written: 'You shall worship the Lord, your God, and him alone shall you serve.'"

Then he led him to Jerusalem, made him stand on the parapet of the temple, and said to him, "If you are the Son of God, throw yourself down from here, for it is written:

'He will command his angels concerning you, to guard you,' and: 'With their hands they will support you, lest you dash your foot against a stone.'"

Jesus said to him in reply, "It also says, 'You shall not put the Lord, your God, to the test.'" When the devil had finished every temptation, he departed from him for a time.

Appreciating the Word

 After a moment of silent reflection, another member of the group reads the following commentary.

At his baptism in the Jordan River, the Spirit of God came down upon Jesus as the voice of God proclaimed, "This is my beloved Son." The Spirit of God then led Jesus into the desert, a place where he would not have chosen to spend forty days and nights. There the Spirit of God led Jesus to confront the devil and his temptations. There the Spirit of God led Jesus to reflect on who he was. There, in the desert, the Spirit of God led Jesus to consider his mission and ministry.

That same Spirit of God now leads us into the desert, not a desert of blazing sun and scorching heat, but a desert made up of the forty days of Lent. It is in this Lenten desert that the Spirit of God challenges us to reflect on our life just as the Spirit of God led Jesus to reflect on his life and mission as he faced temptation. In this Lenten desert the Spirit leads us to examine whether we are faithfully living out the promises of our baptism—promises to turn from sin and selfishness and to move away from those things, persons, and behaviors that hinder us from following Christ.

As the Spirit of God led Jesus into the desert and guided him throughout his ministry, so that same Spirit of God brings us to another season of Lent. If we are open to the Spirit of God, that Spirit will lead us to greater joy and deeper holiness, that Spirit will lead us into the very heart of God.

Reflecting on My Life

- What word or sentence in the Gospel speaks to you?

The First Reading

In Deuteronomy 26:4–10, Moses tells the people how they are to offer praise and thanks to God for the wonders God has worked for them. This reading can bring to mind the Liturgy of the Eucharist during which we present our gifts to the Lord and we declare the wonders God has worked for us in Jesus, his Son.

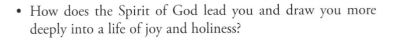

- How does the Spirit of God lead you and draw you more deeply into a life of joy and holiness?

- What is your goal for this Lent? Why?

 Write it down!

This week, observe ways that you are led by the Spirit of God though various activities and choices throughout the day. Spend a few minutes jotting them down here.

Reflecting on My Home

- What can you do to make Lent a sacred time at home?

• How might you involve other family or household members in an active Lent?

The Second Reading

In Romans 10:8–13, Paul declares that all who proclaim Jesus as Lord, Jew or Greek, will be saved. Paul leads us to see that God's salvation goes beyond the boundaries we may impose.

Reflecting on My Parish

• In what ways does the worship life of the parish keep you focused on the Lord?

• What opportunities does the parish offer to help you enter more deeply into the life of God? Which do you take advantage of?

Affecting My World

 Choose a good work to do for Lent:

- Contact your social concerns committee and volunteer to serve in a soup kitchen.
- Contact your local senior center or nursing home to see how you might help out.
- As a group, sacrifice a cup of coffee or snack each day and donate the money to a specific charity, such as Food for the Poor, to be collected and pooled at the end of Lent.
- Visit Catholic Charities USA (www.catholiccharities.org) and click on *Poverty Facts* to educate yourself about poverty in the United States and policies of the Church in response.
- Visit the website (www.usccb.org) to learn about a wide variety of issues and what you can do to help.

Sending Forth

Leader   Let us take a moment of quiet prayer,
              listening to the Spirit of God
              so that we might enter fully into this season of Lent

              Pause for silent prayer.

              We pray:

All   Spirit of God, lead us to new life.

Leader   Help us to turn away from sin and to reform our lives.

All   Spirit of God, lead us to new life.

Leader   Keep us mindful of all the ways we can serve our
              brothers and sisters.

All   Spirit of God, lead us to new life.

Leader   Let us pray for particular people and needs.

              *Please name specific people and any special concerns
              needing prayer.*

All   Loving God,
you give us this season of Lent
so that we may take time to consider
how we are faithfully living out
the promises of our baptism.
We ask you to be with us as we begin our Lenten
journey.
Amen.

Week Two: Shining Divinely

READINGS FOR THE SECOND SUNDAY
OF LENT:
- Genesis 15:5–12, 17–18
- Philippians 3:17–4:1
- Luke 9:28–36

Setting the Environment

 On a table in the center of your group, place a Lenten colored cloth, a bible, an artistic representation of Christ, a votive candle for each member of the group, and a single lit taper candle from which to light the votives.

Gathering Prayer

Leader   Transforming God,
           you are our light and our salvation.

           Pause to light each votive candle.

           Let us pray.

All   Be with us as we break open the Word.
           Change our hearts that your radiance may shine
           through us so that all may see your glory and
           know your powerful love.
           We ask this in Jesus' name.
           Amen.

Connecting with Life

 The facilitator or another member of the group reads aloud the following introduction then introduces the discussion questions that follow it.

Even people we think we know can surprise us. They can do something we don't expect. They can reveal a talent we never knew they had, express a surprising opinion, or enjoy a style of music we would never have imagined being on their iPod. People are always—at least in part—a mystery. That's what makes marriage, friendship, parenthood, or any other long-term relationship a continuing discovery. Each party continues to learn more about the other. And sometimes that discovery comes unexpectedly. You may walk into a friend's workplace and realize for the first time the highly respected executive position that person holds. You accompany your spouse to his or her high school reunion, and you realize your partner was the most popular graduate in recent years. An emergency arises, and you watch with amazement as the quiet person you thought you knew, suddenly springs into action and takes charge. People can surprise us!

- Describe a time when someone you thought you knew, did something surprising or out of character.

- Have you ever surprised yourself by something that popped out of your mouth or by something you suddenly found yourself doing in an unexpected situation? What happened?

Listening to the Word

 Take a quiet moment to pray a prayer such as, "O Lord, be in our minds, in our hearts, and on our lips that we might listen fully to your Word."

A member of the group then reads aloud the Gospel for the Second Sunday of Lent, using the bible from the table in the center of the group.

Gospel Reading: Luke 9:28b–36

Jesus took Peter, John, and James and went up the mountain to pray. While he was praying his face changed in appearance and his clothing became dazzling white. And behold, two men were conversing with him, Moses and Elijah, who appeared in glory and spoke of his exodus that he was going to accomplish in Jerusalem. Peter and his companions had been overcome by sleep, but becoming fully awake, they saw his glory and the two men standing with him. As they were about to part from him, Peter said to Jesus, "Master, it is good that we are here; let us make three tents, one for you, one for Moses, and one for Elijah." But he did not know what he was saying. While he was still speaking, a cloud came and cast a shadow over them, and they became frightened when they entered the cloud.

Then from the cloud came a voice that said, "This is my chosen Son; listen to him." After the voice had spoken, Jesus was found alone. They fell silent and did not at that time tell anyone what they had seen.

Appreciating the Word

 After a moment of silent reflection, another group member reads the following commentary.

Jesus took Peter, James, and John with him as he went up on the mountain and was transfigured in glory. There Jesus more clearly revealed who he was. He was God's beloved Son, shining with divinity. He was the fulfillment of the law and the prophets as represented by Moses and Elijah. Peter, James, and John certainly got a better understanding of who their master was. He was far more than the teacher, the rabbi, and the worker of miracles they had supposed him to be.

This season of Lent not only challenges us to grow in our appreciation and understanding of Jesus, it also challenges us to consider who we truly are. We are God's children made so in the sacrament of baptism where God claimed us as his own. We are part of God's Church. We are brothers and sisters in Christ and his living presence in the world.

And we are to live and act in such a way that the world may come to know us for who we truly are. We are to live in such a way that the goodness of God, the holiness of God, and the compassion of God may be seen in our lives.

In his moment of transfiguration, Peter, James, and John discovered more about Jesus. This Lent, may people discover more about us as faithful followers of Christ!

Reflecting on My Life

• What word or sentence in the Gospel speaks to you?

- What do you suppose the apostles were thinking when they saw the transformation of Jesus?

- What in your life needs transformation so that you can be a more faithful follower of Christ?

 Write it down!
Take time to journal each day this coming week. Here are some questions to get you started:

- What needs transformation in my life?

- In what ways have I allowed God to transform me this day?

The First Reading

In Genesis 15:5–12, 17–18, Abraham experiences the awesome presence of God, who chooses to make a covenant with him.

Reflecting on My Parish

- The parish community strengthens us on the journey to deeper holiness and commitment to our baptismal promises. How are you supported by your parish community?

- What more could it do?

- Describe a significant time when you felt the strength of the parish as a community. For example, was there a particular worship service, retreat, social event, or outreach to a person or an organization in need?

Reflecting on My Home

- Discuss how you know when God is speaking to you in the everyday tasks and activities of your life. Can you give examples?

- What can you do to be aware of God in each family or household member this week?

Affecting My World

 Commit yourself to a service for someone else and notice how a simple action transforms you or the other:

- Run an errand for an elderly neighbor.
- Call a family member that you haven't spoken to for awhile.
- Contact your parish social concerns committee, St. Vincent de Paul ministries, or diocesan Catholic Charities to see where you are needed.
- Contact Catholic Relief Services (CRS) so that you might contribute to emergency needs by engaging other parish groups to help. Catholic Relief Services, 228 W. Lexington St., Baltimore, Maryland 21201-3413; 888-277-7575; www.crs.org.

The Second Reading

In Philippians 3:17–4:1, Paul speaks of the future God has in store for those who stand firm in the Lord. We are to live conscious that that our citizenship is in heaven.

Sending Forth

Leader   Let us take a moment of quiet prayer, listening to all that the Spirit of God has spoken to us in our sharing.

Pause for silent prayer.

We pray:

All   **God of Light, Change us!
Give us the courage to be transformed in your image and likeness that we might bring light to a world grown weary of empty dreams and broken promises.**

Leader   The Lord is my light and my salvation.

All   **The Lord is the stronghold of my life.**

Leader   We go forth in joy and hope.

All   **To serve our God and each other.**

⚘| Week Three: Investing in God

READINGS FOR THE THIRD SUNDAY
OF LENT:
- Exodus 3:1–8a, 13–5
- 1 Corinthians 10:1–6, 10–12
- Luke 13:1–9

Note: In some parishes the Gospel from Cycle A about the Samaritan woman (John 4:5–42) will be heard rather than the reading included here. This is permitted, especially where there are catechumens present, because of its importance to Christian initiation.

Setting the Environment

On a table in the center of your group, place a Lenten cloth and a symbol of fruitfulness: a plant, a bowl of grapes or figs, a mini bonsai tree, a pruning tool, along with a bible and a lighted candle. Additionally, you will need to recruit a leader and five readers for the Gathering Prayer.

Gathering Prayer

Leader   Let us begin by silently acknowledging that we are always in the presence of our loving God.

Pause for silent prayer.

Powerful God,
We praise you, for you are kind and merciful.

Reader 1   Bless the Lord, O my soul.
All my being, bless his holy name.

Reader 2   Bless the Lord, O my soul,
            And forget not all his benefits.

Reader 3   He pardons all your iniquities,
            he heals all your sins.

Reader 4   Bless the Lord, O my soul.
            Merciful and gracious is the Lord,
            slow to anger and abounding in kindness.

Reader 5   For as high as the heavens are above the earth,
            so surpassing is his kindness to those who fear
            him.

            Bless the Lord, O my soul.
            All my being, bless his holy name.

Connecting with Life

 The facilitator or another member of the group reads aloud the following introduction then introduces the discussion questions that follow it.

All of us are investors. Some people buy stocks and bonds. Some people put their cash into bank accounts or certificates of deposit. Some purchase real estate while others convert their assets into silver or gold. Some people buy and sell commodities like oil and natural gas.

But whether or not we make investments like those just mentioned, all of us are investors. We invest in our relationships; giving our hearts to persons we love. We invest time and energy in organizations whose goals we admire; we give them financial support. We invest in movements whose ideals are like our own and we stand behind them. We invest in our physical health and well-being: we exercise, eat right, and go to the doctor. We invest in our intellectual growth: we read, take courses, or pursue advanced degrees.

We make the investments we do because we expect a return. We expect our financial wealth to increase. Or we expect our physical, emotional, or intellectual life to improve. Or we expect society to move in a more positive direction. We all invest in various people, organizations, processes, or activities, and we all expect a positive return on the investments we make.

- Share about a time when someone made an investment in you or in an idea or project you were promoting.

- Have you ever invested in a personal relationship and had your investment pay off in a wonderful way?

Listening to the Word

 Take a quiet moment to pray a prayer such as, "O Lord, be in our minds, in our hearts, and on our lips that we might listen fully to your Word."

A member of the group then reads aloud the Gospel for the Third Sunday of Lent, using the bible from the table in the center of the group.

Gospel Reading: Luke 13:1–9

Some people who were present there told Jesus about the Galileans whose blood Pilate had mingled with the blood of their sacrifices. He said to them in reply, "Do you think that because these Galileans suffered in this way they were greater sinners than all other Galileans? By no means! But I tell you, if you do not repent, you will all perish as they did! Or those eighteen people who were killed when the tower at Siloam fell on them—do you think they were more guilty than everyone else who lived in Jerusalem? By no means! But I tell you, if you do not repent, you will all perish as they did!"

And he told them this parable: "There once was a person who had a fig tree planted in his orchard, and when he came in search of fruit on it but found none, he said to the gardener, 'For three years now I have come in search of fruit on this fig tree but have found none. (So) cut it down. Why should it exhaust the soil?' He [the gardener] said to him in reply, 'Sir, leave it for this year also, and I shall cultivate the ground around it and fertilize it; it may bear fruit in the future. If not you can cut it down.'"

Appreciating the Word

After a moment of silent reflection, another member of the group reads the following commentary.

Jesus told of a man who came looking for fruit on his fig tree. Finding none, he decided to have the tree cut down. His gardener persuaded the owner to give the tree another year. With further cultivation and fertilizer that barren tree might yet become fruitful.

We are like that fig tree. God has planted us in this world and God expects us to be fruitful. God expects us to bear the fruit of charity, kindness, forgiveness, and compassion. God expects us to help bring forth his kingdom of love, justice, and peace.

However, as this Lenten season reminds us, we often fall short in bearing the fruit we should. We sin, we fail, we are overly self-concerned, and selfish. We pray in the Confiteor at Mass, "I confess to Almighty God and to you my brothers and sisters that I have sinned through my own fault, in what I have done and in what I have failed to do." In other words, we sometimes show little return on the investment God has made in us.

But God does not cut us down. Instead, God gives us another chance to bear fruit, another chance to hear and answer Lent's call to "turn away from sin and be faithful to the Gospel," as we hear when our foreheads are marked with ashes on Ash Wednesday. To help us do that, the Lord cultivates and fertilizes us so that we might produce the good fruit that he expects of us.

The Lord Jesus cultivates us by making us part of the rough and tumble life of his Church, by challenging us in the sacrament of penance, and by opening our minds and hearts to the needs of others.

The Lord fertilizes and nourishes us through his Word in scripture, through the sacred bread and wine of the Eucharist, through his gentle presence in prayer, and through our fellow Christians who support and encourage us.

Like us, God is an investor. And like us, God expects a good return!

Reflecting on My Life

- What word or sentence in the Gospel speaks to you?

- How has the Word of God borne fruit in your life?

The First Reading

In Exodus 3:1–8a, God tells Moses that he has seen the suffering of his people in Egypt and that he is about to rescue them. As a sign of investing his love in them, God reveals his name to Moses. "I AM" sends Moses to the Israelites to lead them to the Promised Land.

- Have you ever felt a time of barrenness in prayer? Why did that change for you?

- How does God tend to you as a faithful gardener would tend his or her garden?

Write it down!

Reflect on how God has taken root in your life. In the space below or in your journal, draw a plant or a vine representing the strength of God in your life and write a prayer of thanksgiving.

Reflecting on My Home

- What things do you grow or create at home? Talk about that process in terms of your family or household investments and returns. What do you collectively put into the process and what do you get out of it?

- How is that investment like your relationship with God?

Reflecting on My Parish

- What are some ways that the parish nourishes the Word of God in you? In what ways does it help you bear good fruit?

The Second Reading

In 1 Corinthians 10:1–6, 10–12, Paul reminds his readers that even though God bestowed his blessings on the Israelites, they sinned. They failed to bear the good fruit God expected of them. The punishment they suffered ought to serve as an example and a warning to us.

- In what ways is your parish providing a good return on its investments in the work of God's kingdom?

Affecting My World

- Buy a seed starter kit—flower or vegetable—from your local garden center and watch it begin to grow. Reflect on or discuss with other family or household members how caring for the plant is like God caring for you. Talk about ways to care for each other.
- Bring a plant to a friend or a person who needs some cheer. Express to them in a note or conversation how they are like a flourishing plant in God's eyes. Tell them how you benefit from the good fruit (kindness, generosity, patience, etc.) they produce.

- Contact your parish or civic "green" or Earth Day committee to see how you can be involved in a planting program this spring.
- Contact Heifer International to see how you can help people in need. You can donate funds toward heifers, ducks, llamas, chickens, and more. Check out how to donate and their gift catalogue at www.heifer.org.
- Consider investing in companies that have green policies and projects.
- Buy Fair Trade coffee and other products at www .fairtradecoffee.org to support farmers in developing countries.

Sending Forth

Leader   Let us take a moment of quiet prayer, listening to all the Spirit of God has spoken to us in our sharing.

Pause for silent prayer.

Powerful God,
You continually call us to newness of life.

All   Nourish us that we may turn away from sin.
May we grow strong and bear fruit that will last so all people will know you by the way we live. This we ask in the name of Jesus, our Lord and brother who lives and reigns with you, now and forever.
Amen.

Leader   Let us go forth to continue our Lenten journey.

All   Amen.

 # Week Four: Love Unconditionally

READINGS FOR THE FOURTH SUNDAY
OF LENT
- Joshua 5:9a, 10–12
- 2 Corinthians 5:17–21
- Luke 15:1–3, 11–32

Note: In some parishes the Gospel from Cycle A about the man born blind (John 9:1–41) will be heard rather than the reading included here. This is permitted, especially where there are catechumens present, because of its importance to Christian initiation.

Setting the Environment

 Along with a lighted candle and a bible on a table covered in purple, place a news photo (or photos) of a significant local or world event that cries out for love, forgiveness, reconciliation, or prayer.
* For the Sending Forth prayer, you will need three readers in addition to the leader.

Gathering Prayer

Leader   We invite you, Loving God, into our hearts.

All   Forgive our sins, our failings, our stubbornness, and hardness of hearts.

Leader   Let us feel your loving presence with us as we break open your Word.

All   Open and change our hearts, Lord.

Connecting with Life

 The facilitator or another member of the group reads aloud the following introduction then introduces the discussion questions that follow it.

Families can be described as intact, blended, nuclear, extended, multi-generational, upper-class, middle-class, lower class, impoverished, educated, un-educated, first-world, second-world, third-world, traditional, non-traditional, and single-parent. The list could obviously go on and on! All these adjectives are designed to help others get a better understanding of the particular family we are describing.

There is another word often used today to describe a family, in fact it is a word used by people to describe their own families and to explain their behavior, and that word is dysfunctional. According to Wikipedia, "a dysfunctional family is a family in which conflict, misbehavior, and even abuse on the part of individual members of the family occur continually and regularly, leading other members to accommodate such actions."

Or to put it another way, dysfunctional families are those that don't function as expected. They don't follow the behavior patterns of a healthy, well-functioning family, where individual members can appropriately thrive.

- How would you describe the family in which you grew up? How is your present family the same or different from your family of origin?

• Describe the positive traits you see in your family today.

Listening to the Word

 Take a quiet moment to pray a prayer such as, "O Lord, be in our minds, in our hearts, and on our lips that we might listen fully to your Word."
A member of the group then reads aloud the Gospel for the Fourth Sunday of Lent, using the bible from the table in the center of the group.

Gospel Reading: Luke 15:1–3, 11–32

Tax collectors and sinners were all drawing near to listen to him, but the Pharisees and scribes began to complain, saying, "This man welcomes sinners and eats with them." So to them he addressed this parable.

"A man had two sons, and the younger son said to his father,

'Father, give me the share of your estate that should come to me.' So the father divided the property between them. After a few days, the younger son collected all his belongings and set off to a distant country where he squandered his inheritance on a life of dissipation. When he had freely spent everything, a severe famine struck that country, and he found himself in dire need. So he hired himself out to one of the local citizens who sent him to his farm to tend the swine. And he longed to eat his fill of the pods on which the swine fed, but nobody gave him any. Coming to his senses he thought, 'How many of my father's hired workers have more than enough food to eat, but here am I, dying from hunger. I shall get up and go to my father and I shall say to him, "Father, I have sinned against heaven and against you. I no longer deserve to be called your son; treat me as you would treat one of your hired workers."' So he got up and went back to his father. While he was still a long way off, his father caught sight of him, and was filled with compassion. He ran to his son, embraced him and kissed him. His son said to him, 'Father, I have sinned against heaven and against you; I no longer deserve to be called your son.'

But his father ordered his servants, 'Quickly bring the finest robe and put it on him; put a ring on his finger and sandals on his feet. Take the fattened calf and slaughter it. Then let us celebrate with a feast, because this son of mine was dead, and has come to life again; he was lost, and has been found.' Then the celebration began.

Now the older son had been out in the field and, on his way back, as he neared the house, he heard the sound of music and dancing. He called one of the servants and asked what this might mean. The servant said to him, 'Your brother has returned and your father has slaughtered the fattened calf because he has him back safe and sound.'

He became angry, and when he refused to enter the house, his father came out and pleaded with him. He said to his father in reply, 'Look, all these years I served you and not once did I disobey your orders; yet you never gave me even a young goat to feast on with my friends. But when your son returns who swallowed up your property with prostitutes, for him you slaughter the fattened calf.' His father said to him, 'My son, you are here with me always; everything I have is yours. But now we must celebrate and rejoice, because your brother was dead and has come to life again; he was lost and has been found.'"

Appreciating the Word

In the Gospel reading for the Fourth Sunday of Lent, Jesus tells the parable of the Prodigal Son, a parable that might also be called that of the Forgiving Father. In that parable we meet a family that could be described as dysfunctional. There is a father

The First Reading

In Joshua 5: 9a, 10–12, we hear how the Israelites celebrate the Passover in the Promised Land. With God's help, they have passed from a land of slavery to a land of freedom. Our journey through Lent mirrors this passage from the slavery of sin to the freedom of God's children.

raising two grown sons who are still at home. No mother is mentioned. Has she died? Been sent away? Or is she so little respected as to not be worthy of mention by the three men of the family?

The father loves his sons, but he seems to be overly indulgent to the younger and seemingly distant from the older. When the younger son demands his inheritance and in essence tells his father he does not have time to wait for him to die, the father gives that son what he wants. When the son returns home, broken and broke, the father treats him like a returning hero. The father lavishes him with gifts and a party rather than with the punishment and scorn he so rightly deserves.

The younger son is selfish, self-absorbed, and interested only in fulfilling his every desire. He has no concern for how his leaving will affect the family and no concern for his family obligations or for the feelings of his father or his older brother.

The older son is obedient but resentful. He does what he must out of a sense of obligation but not out of love. He refers to his younger brother as his father's son rather than as "my brother." He keeps his brother at a distance and refuses to approve of the mercy and forgiveness his father is willing to show the younger son.

In this parable of a seemingly dysfunctional family, we learn something of God's forgiveness. We are God's children—sons and daughters who do not live up to our baptismal responsibilities. We sin, we move away from God. But when we come to our senses and return to the Lord, he welcomes us, no questions asked. He clothes us with grace and welcomes us back to his table. We have a God who loves us unconditionally despite our failings and sins. He loved humanity so much that he humbled himself to bring us home as he took on flesh in the person of Jesus Christ.

If our self-righteousness blinds us to our own sin, if we resent the mercy he shows to those we label as lost, he humbles himself to come out to meet us. He reaches out in word and sacrament; he showers us with his love and grace.

Today's parable proclaims that when it comes to his children, God does not act as we would expect. God does not act with logic and justice but rather with undeserved and unmerited forgiveness and love.

Reflecting on My Life

- What word or sentence in the Gospel speaks to you?

- Have you ever felt totally and unconditionally loved? Describe.

- When have you had the opportunity to forgive someone? Why
did you do it?

The Second Reading

In 2 Corinthians 5:17–21,
Paul reminds us that in
Christ we have been rec-
onciled to God. We have
become a new creation. As
people forgiven by God, we
are to be agents of forgiveness and reconciliation in
our world.

- How did it change you and the
other person?

Write it down!

*Is there someone you need to forgive or ask forgiveness of?
Make a fresh start this week toward that goal. Jot down
what you will do to begin the process.*

Reflecting on My Home

- Describe how you, your family, or members of your household share love with each other even after being hurt.

- What do you do to make up?

Reflecting on My Parish

- How is your parish community welcoming to newcomers, strangers, and immigrants?

- What more could it do?

Affecting My World

- Go out of your way for the sake of another person this week.
- Spend quality time with your family, friends, and loved ones this week.
- Discover where there is a parish, community, or world situation that needs help immediately. How can you help address that need?
- Contact Bread for the World (www.bread.org) to see how you can contribute to their work against world hunger.
- Check out the Catholic Home Missions section of the United States Conference of Catholic Bishops' web site (www.usccb.org). Catholic Home Missions is the name for dioceses and parishes in the United States that cannot provide basic pastoral services like Mass and the other sacraments; religious education; ministry training for priests, deacons, religious sisters, and lay people; and outreach to the poor. See how you might help. Contact: homemissions@usccb.org.

Sending Forth

Leader   Let us take a moment of quiet prayer, listening to all the Spirit of God has spoken to us in our sharing.

Pause for silent prayer.

Let us pray together the beautiful Responsorial Psalm from the Fourth Sunday of Lent.

From Psalm 34

All   Taste and see the goodness of the Lord.

Reader 1   I will bless the LORD at all times;
           praise shall be always in my mouth.
           My soul will glory in the LORD
           that the poor may hear and be glad.

All   Taste and see the goodness of the Lord.

Reader 2   Magnify the LORD with me;
           let us exalt his name together.
           I sought the LORD, who answered me, delivered me
           from all my fears.

All   Taste and see the goodness of the Lord.

Reader 3   Look to God that you may be radiant with joy and
           your faces may not blush for shame.
           In my misfortune I called, the LORD heard
           and saved me from all distress.

Leader   Let us go forth to love unconditionally.

All   Amen.

NOTE: See Setting the Environment for next week's meeting where you are asked to display photos of yourselves and influential people in your lives.

Week Five: Look Beyond

READINGS FOR THE FIFTH SUNDAY
OF LENT
- Isaiah 43:16–21
- Philippians 3:8–14
- John 8:1–11

 NOTE: In some parishes the Gospel from Cycle A about the raising of Lazarus (John 11:1–45) will be heard rather than the reading included here. This is permitted, especially where there are catechumens present, because of its importance to Christian initiation.

Setting the Environment

 On a table covered with a Lenten colored cloth, place a lighted candle, a bible, and favorite photos of yourselves from your past and photos or names of persons who believed in you or influenced you for good.

Gathering Prayer

Leader   The Lord has done great things for us!

All   We are filled with great joy.

Leader   Bless our gathering as we seek to hear you in our prayer.
Open our hearts as you call us to continuing growth and newness.

All   May we embrace the gifts you give us
             so that we may grow as your disciples
             to serve our brothers and sisters.
             Amen.

Connecting with Life

 *The facilitator or another member of the group reads aloud
the following introduction then introduces the discussion
questions that follow it.*

High school reunions are attended by some people and avoided by many others. Those who avoid them are those not particularly interested in remembering or reliving their years in high school.

For many people being a freshman, sophomore, junior, and senior—being an adolescent—was not the easiest time in life. There were outbreaks of acne, bouts of confusion, feelings of worthlessness, over or under physical development, comparisons with others, and thinking that everyone was secure and accepted but you. There was the cruelty of classmates, all too ready to pick on others to avoid being the object of cruel jokes themselves. And of course there was the labeling of people as jocks or geeks, winners or losers, popular or pathetic, etc., and there was little way of escaping your "box" once you had been labeled and put in your place.

For many people the years of high school were painful and challenging. Such people are not ready to relive them at a reunion where people often revert to roles long forgotten. People grow and change. People break out of their boxes and pull off the labels stuck on them by others. Many people leave the past behind, and often for good reason.

• Share a positive way in which you have changed since your years in high school.

- Do you let people move beyond their past, or do you tend to see them in the same way you first categorized them?

Listening to the Word

 Take a quiet moment to pray a prayer such as, "O Lord, be in our minds, in our hearts, and on our lips that we might listen fully to your Word."

A member of the group then reads aloud the Gospel for the Fifth Sunday of Lent, using the bible from the table in the center of the group.

Gospel Reading: John 8:1–11

Jesus went to the Mount of Olives. But early in the morning he arrived again in the temple area, and all the people started coming to him, and he sat down and taught them. Then the scribes and the Pharisees brought a woman who had been caught in adultery and made her stand in the middle. They said to him, "Teacher, this woman was caught in the very act of committing adultery. Now in the law, Moses commanded us to stone such women. So what do you say?" They said this to test him, so that they could have some charge to bring against him.

Jesus bent down and began to write on the ground with his finger. But when they continued asking him, he straightened up and said to them, "Let the one among you who is without sin be the first to throw a stone at her." Again he bent down and wrote on the ground. And in response, they went away one by one, beginning with the elders. So he was left alone with the woman before him. Then Jesus straightened up and said to her, "Woman, where are they? Has no one condemned you?" She replied, "No one, sir." Then Jesus said, "Neither do I condemn you. Go, [and] from now on do not sin any more."

Appreciating the Word

 After a moment of silent reflection, another member of the group reads the following commentary.

Looking at the Gospel reading for this Fifth Sunday of Lent, we might conclude that Jesus was not particularly interested in another person's past. In the passage, a woman whose recent past had included an incident of adultery, an incident that could very well have been the latest in a string of such sexual encounters, is dragged before Jesus. And what does he do? He begins "to write on the ground with his finger."

I have always been intrigued by what Jesus might have written on the ground that caused those who dragged the woman before Jesus to drift away. Did he write the sins of the woman's accusers on the ground—in the sight of all? Did he write out passages from the scriptures dealing with God's mercy and forgiveness? Did he simply write on the ground to give himself time to think of what he should do? Of course, he could have done any of those things, but perhaps what Jesus did was simply to doodle on the ground because he was disinterested in what was being said. Jesus doodled just like we do when we are stuck in a boring class or meeting or when someone talks away on the phone about something in which we have no interest at all.

Jesus was not interested in the woman's past. Yes, she had sinned. That was her past. Jesus was concerned with the woman's future, in what she could become. That's why he said, "Neither do I condemn you. Go, and from now on do not sin any more."

In this season of Lent we rejoice that we have a God who calls us not to have a reunion with our past with its sins and failings, but rather to look forward to what we can become with his mercy and grace. As we were told on Ash Wednesday, "turn away from sin and be faithful to the Gospel." Don't be held bound and condemned by your past, but embrace the present and future as your time to change and become the Christian you were meant to be!

Reflecting on My Life

- What word or sentence in the Gospel speaks to you?

The First Reading

In Isaiah 43:16–21, God tells the exiles in Babylon that he will do wonderful things for them just as he did for the Chosen People in bringing them out of slavery in Egypt. God's wonders are not just past events but a cause for future hope.

- What do you imagine was in the woman's heart when Jesus said, "Neither do I condemn you. Go, and from now on do not sin any more"?

- How do you know God's love even when you sin?

 Write it down!

There are things in life that we all regret—an unkindness, a malicious word or thought, or other actions we are ashamed of. Have you allowed God to forgive you for these acts? Pray about it this week and notice how God has forgiven you.

Reflecting on My Home

- Sometimes we have disputes or disagreements with other family members. It's normal. How do you forgive or ask forgiveness afterwards?

- Take some time to tell the good qualities that you see in each other.

The Second Reading

In Phillippians 3:8–14, Paul proclaims that the loss of all things means nothing in comparison to knowing Christ. Paul pushes forward to what lies ahead for those faithful to the Lord.

Reflecting on My Parish

- As a parish community, how can we respect others by rising above judgments and stereotypes in order to be more understanding and welcoming?

- Are there situations in our neighborhood or world community that call us to take a stand for others?

Affecting My World

- Take time to read your local community paper and see if there is a need that you might help out with.
- Get involved with a building project or clothing or food drive to benefit people in need.
- Visit a homeless shelter and talk to people there about their situations.
- Invite a newcomer in your neighborhood or workplace for coffee.
- Meet a person who is a recent immigrant and ask how they are doing and see if there is something you can help them with.
- Contact Habitat for Humanity (www.habitat.org) and click on *Volunteer Locally* to see what projects are in your area that you might help with.

Sending Forth

Leader   Let us take a moment of quiet prayer,
          listening to all that the Spirit of God has spoken to us
          in our sharing.

          Pause for silent prayer.

          The Lord says, "See, I am doing something new! Now it springs forth,
          Do you not perceive it?"

All   **The Lord had done great things for us; we are filled with joy!**

Leader   We ask God to hear our prayers for people who have influenced us and helped us to grow.

          Group members may share names out loud or in silence.

          For all of these, we offer thanksgiving as we pray the prayer that Jesus taught us.

All   **Our Father . . .**

Leader   Loving God,
           we turn away from our old lives of sin
           and turn to the new life of goodness and grace.
           Help us not to be judges but healers;
           To be people of hospitality rather than gatekeepers;
           To be people of compassion rather than condemnation,
           and people of justice rather than discrimination.
           We ask this through Jesus Christ our Lord and brother.

All   Amen.

Leader   Let us go forth to live what we believe!

All   Amen!

 NOTE: Next Sunday is Palm Sunday when the Gospel reading is the Passion narrative from Luke's Gospel. We've included a shortened version here for the group meeting. However, group members may want read the entire passage in preparation for the meeting and so citation is given for that as well. Discuss and decide what you will do with your group before you end this week's session.

Week Six: Faithful to the Mission

READINGS FOR PASSION SUNDAY
- Isaiah 50:4–7
- Philippians 2:6–11
- Luke 22:14–23:56 (Complete text)

Setting the Environment

 On a table covered with a red cloth, place a bible and symbols of Palm (Passion) Sunday and Holy Week. For example place palm branches, an artistic representation of Jesus entering Jerusalem, a crucifix, crown of thorns, or other appropriate symbols.

Gathering Prayer

 Taize album Laudate, Music of Taize *or similar appropriate music. After a few reflective minutes, the leader begins.*

Leader	We begin our prayer † In the name of the Father, and of the Son, and of the Holy Spirit. Blessed is the King who comes in the name of the Lord.
All	Peace in heaven and glory in the highest.
Leader	Ever faithful God, as we prepare for this most solemn of weeks, increase our faith and our faithfulness.
All	We believe in your promise of new life. May we give ourselves as fully as you did. Amen.

Connecting with Life

 The facilitator or another member of the group reads aloud the following introduction then introduces the discussion questions that follow it.

One of the harsh lessons we learn growing up is that people don't always keep their promises. People are not always faithful to the words they speak and the commitments they make.

A parent tells a child that the family will visit Disney World next summer. But when the economy tanks and the family has to conserve, plans change. Yet all the child knows is that a commitment was made and broken. The complaints begin "but you promised!"

At school, children make friends, good friends, even best friends. Promises written in yearbooks declare that those friendships will last forever. But "friends forever" seldom proves true. School friendships more often than not become distant memories.

At work, employers tell their workers that their salaries are secure and their jobs are safe. But as the recent global economic downturn painfully demonstrated, such promises and assurances can be quite deceptive, lulling us into a false sense of security.

On their wedding day, the bride and groom promise they will love and honor each other for the rest of their lives. But if couples were faithful to their commitments, there would be no need for divorce lawyers and marriage tribunals.

Candidates running for office leave a trail of promises as they go. But, as the electorate sadly knows, when candidates win, something happens. Campaign promises are often set aside in order to gain greater political leverage on the immediate agenda. Candidates often prove unfaithful to their words.

- Share your earliest memory of a promise that was made to you and not kept.

- When it comes to keeping promises, how faithful are you?

Listening to the Word

 Take a quiet moment to pray a prayer such as, "O Lord, be in our minds, in our hearts, and on our lips that we might listen fully to your Word."

A member or several members of the group then read(s) aloud the Passion narrative, using the bible from the table in the center of the group.

Condensed Gospel Reading: Luke 22:14–23:25

When the hour came, Jesus took his place at table with the apostles. He said to them, "I have eagerly desired to eat this Passover with you before I suffer, for, I tell you, I shall not eat it (again) until there is fulfillment in the kingdom of God." Then he took a cup, gave thanks, and said, "Take this and share it among yourselves; for I tell you (that) from this time on I shall not drink of the fruit of the vine until the kingdom of God comes." Then he took the bread, said the blessing, broke it, and gave it to them, saying, "This is my body, which will be given for you; do this in memory of me." And likewise the cup after they had eaten, saying, "This cup is the new covenant in my blood, which will be shed for you."

"And yet behold, the hand of the one who is to betray me is with me on the table; for the Son of Man indeed goes as it has been determined; but woe to that man by whom he is betrayed." And they began to debate among themselves who among them would do such a deed.

Then an argument broke out among them about which of them should be regarded as the greatest. He said to them, "The kings of the Gentiles lord it over them and those in authority over them are addressed as 'Benefactors'; but among you it shall not be so. Rather, let the greatest among you be as the youngest, and the leader as the servant. For who is greater: the one seated at table or the one who serves? Is it not the one seated at table? I am among you as the one who serves. It is you who have stood by me in my trials; and I confer a kingdom on you, just as my Father has conferred one on me, that you may eat and drink at my table in my kingdom; and you will sit on thrones judging the twelve tribes of Israel.

"Simon, Simon, behold Satan has demanded to sift all of you like wheat, but I have prayed that your own faith may not fail; and once you have turned back, you must strengthen your brothers." Peter said to him, "Lord, I am prepared to go to prison and to die with you." But he replied, "I tell you, Peter, before the cock crows this day, you will deny three times that you know me."

He said to them, "When I sent you forth without a money bag or a sack or sandals, were you in need of anything?" "No, nothing," they replied. He said to them, "But now one who has a money bag should take it, and likewise a sack, and one who does not have a sword should sell his cloak and buy one. For I tell you that this scripture must be fulfilled in me, namely, 'He was counted among the wicked'; and indeed what is written about me is coming to fulfillment." Then they said, "Lord, look, there are two swords here." But he replied, "It is enough!"

Then going out he went, as was his custom, to the Mount of Olives, and the disciples followed him. When he arrived at the place he said to them, "Pray that you may not undergo the test." After withdrawing about a stone's throw from them and kneeling, he prayed, saying, "Father, if you are willing, take this cup away from me; still, not my will but yours be done." And to strengthen him an angel from heaven appeared to him. He was in such agony and he prayed so fervently that his sweat became like drops of blood falling on the ground. When he rose from prayer and returned to his disciples, he found them sleeping from grief. He said to them, "Why are you sleeping? Get up and pray that you may not undergo the test."

While he was still speaking, a crowd approached and in front was one of the Twelve, a man named Judas. He went up to Jesus to kiss him. Jesus said to him, "Judas, are you betraying the Son of Man with a kiss?" His disciples realized what was about to happen, and they asked, "Lord, shall we strike with a sword?" And one of them struck the high priest's servant and cut off his right ear. But Jesus said in reply, "Stop, no more of this!" Then he touched the servant's ear and healed him. And Jesus said to the chief priests and temple guards and elders who had come for him, "Have you come out as against a robber, with swords and clubs? Day after day I was with you in the temple area, and you did not seize me; but this is your hour, the time for the power of darkness."

After arresting him they led him away and took him into the house of the high priest; Peter was following at a distance. They lit a fire in the middle of the courtyard and sat around it, and Peter sat down with them. When a maid saw him seated in the light, she looked intently at him and said, "This man too was with him." But he denied it saying,

The First Reading

In Isaiah 50:4–7, the prophet Isaiah proclaims that God is his strength. He proclaims God's message despite opposition and suffering. During Holy Week we have the chance to examine deeply to what extent we do likewise.

"Woman, I do not know him." A short while later someone else saw him and said, "You too are one of them"; but Peter answered, "My friend, I am not." About an hour later, still another insisted, "Assuredly, this man too was with him, for he also is a Galilean." But Peter said, "My friend, I do not know what you are talking about." Just as he was saying this, the cock crowed, and the Lord turned and looked at Peter; and Peter remembered the word of the Lord, how he had said to him, "Before the cock crows today, you will deny me three times." He went out and began to weep bitterly. The men who held Jesus in custody were ridiculing and beating him. They blindfolded him and questioned him, saying, "Prophesy! Who is it that struck you?" And they reviled him in saying many other things against him.

When day came the council of elders of the people met, both chief priests and scribes, and they brought him before their Sanhedrin. They said, "If you are the Messiah, tell us," but he replied to them, "If I tell you, you will not believe, and if I question, you will not respond. But from this time on the Son of Man will be seated at the right hand of the power of God." They all asked, "Are you then the Son of God?" He replied to them, "You say that I am." Then they said,

"What further need have we for testimony? We have heard it from his own mouth."

Then the whole assembly of them arose and brought him before Pilate. They brought charges against him, saying, "We found this man misleading our people; he opposes the payment of taxes to Caesar and maintains that he is the Messiah, a king." Pilate asked him, "Are you the king of the Jews?" He said to him in reply, "You say so." Pilate then addressed the chief priests and the crowds, "I find this man not guilty." But they were adamant and said, "He is inciting the people with his teaching throughout all Judea, from Galilee where he began even to here."

On hearing this Pilate asked if the man was a Galilean; and upon learning that he was under Herod's jurisdiction, sent him to Herod who was in Jerusalem at that time.

Herod was very glad to see Jesus; he had been wanting to see him for a long time, for he had heard about him and had been hoping to see him perform some sign. Herod questioned Jesus at length, but he gave no answer. The chief priests and scribes, meanwhile, stood by accusing him harshly. (Even) Herod and his soldiers treated him contemptuously and mocked him, and after clothing him in resplendent garb, he sent him back to Pilate. Herod and Pilate became friends that very day, even though they had been enemies formerly. Pilate then summoned the chief priests, the rulers, and the people and said to them, "You brought this man to me and accused him of inciting the people to revolt. I have conducted my investigation in your presence and have not found this man guilty of the charges you have brought against him, nor did Herod, for he sent him back to us. So no capital crime has been committed by him. Therefore I shall have him flogged and then release him."

But all together they shouted out, "Away with this man! Release Barabbas to us. (Now Barabbas had been imprisoned for a rebellion that had taken place in the city and for murder.) Again Pilate addressed them, still wishing to release Jesus, but they continued their shouting, "Crucify him! Crucify him!" Pilate addressed them a third time, "What evil has this man done? I found him guilty of no capital crime. Therefore I shall have him flogged and then release him." With loud shouts, however, they persisted in calling for his crucifixion, and their voices prevailed. The verdict of Pilate was that their demand should be granted. So he released the man who had been imprisoned for rebellion and murder, for whom they asked, and he handed Jesus over to them to deal with as they wished.

The Second Reading

In Phillippians 2:6–11, Paul tells how Jesus Christ emptied himself for our sake. He humbled himself in service and obedience even to death on a cross. In return God exalted him in glory. In what ways during this past year (since last Holy Week) have you allowed yourself to be humbled in service and obedience to the will of God? In what ways have you known the glory of the resurrection?

Appreciating the Word

After a moment of silent reflection, another member of the group reads the following commentary.

Jesus was a person who was faithful, a person who kept his promises and commitments. Jesus remained faithful to whatever God asked of him. He truly meant and lived what he taught his disciples to say to God, "Thy kingdom come, thy will be done." And because he was faithful, Jesus ended up nailed to a cross.

The faithfulness of Jesus is all the more striking as we read a passion narrative filled with people who were unfaithful to their office and to their promises. There is Judas, the unfaithful friend, who was more committed to money than to his Lord. And Peter, whose words proclaim he is ready to die for his Lord, but who publicly denies him three times.

There are the chief priests and scribes who, rather than faithfully searching the scriptures and exercising their religious authority, turn on Jesus out of jealousy and fear. Then there are Herod and Pilate, civil leaders who knew Jesus had done nothing deserving of death, but are still ready to condemn. Their promise to uphold justice gives way to expediency. And the faithless crowd that turns on Jesus. The king they had welcomed to Jerusalem has become the object of their scorn and derision.

But in this sea of unfaithfulness and broken promises, Jesus remains faithful to who he is, faithful to his mission, faithful to his heavenly Father even through unimaginable suffering and the excruciating pain of the cross. The Father, in turn, remains faithful to Jesus. The resurrection is proof positive of that.

This Passion Sunday we are challenged to consider how faithful, or fickle, or compromising we are when it comes to our commitments to living the Christian life and to the work of Christ's Church.

Reflecting on My Life

- What word or sentence in this account of the Passion speaks to you?

- Jesus suffers and dies for us. What does he ask of us as his followers?

- How does this narrative help you to be a more faithful person—to God, your baptismal call, your family friends, co-workers, and to the mission of Christ?

- How will you spend the Easter Triduum—the three days from sundown on Holy Thursday through sundown on Easter Sunday? How much time for prayer (private and liturgical) and fasting can you manage?

Write it down!

A significant question in Week One was, "What is your goal for this Lent? Why?"

Did you meet your goal? Were you faithful to what you wanted to do? How well did you hear and listen to God speaking to you? Bring this to prayer all week.

Reflecting on My Home

- Discuss and plan how you will participate in the solemn celebrations of the Triduum as a family this week.

- What will you do in your home to make these celebrations significant?

Reflecting on My Parish

- Why is it important that we gather as a parish community to celebrate Holy Week and the resurrection of Jesus?
- After each Mass or service, spend some time in prayer and reflection on how you are strengthened by Word, Eucharist, and community.
- Take a few moments after each celebration to greet people you may not know well. This small step can help connect the community more deeply.

Affecting My World

- Make time this week to stop, pray, reflect on the scriptures and your life.
- Make it a holy week. If possible, take the time off work to attend services.
- Make a sacrifice this week that will help another.
- Offer to bring someone to Holy Week liturgies.
- Volunteer in a place of need this week.

Sending Forth

Leader   Let us take a moment of quiet prayer to thank God
            for all of the gifts of our time together
            as we enter into the solemnity of this coming week,
            knowing the enormity of Christ's love for us.

            Pause for silent prayer.

            Redeeming Lord,
            We walk with you into this week,
            knowing what is to come.

All   You call us to love and faithfulness.

Leader   Let us walk with you as if we were there.

All   You call us to love and faithfulness.

Leader   May we recommit ourselves to faithfulness and
          unrelenting love,

All   **As we strive to remain faithful and, with you,
          serve our brothers and sisters on bended knee.**

Leader   May Almighty God bless us
          as we walk the path to holiness,
          † Father, Son, and Holy Spirit.

All   **Amen.**

Part II:

Weekday Reflections

Connecting with Life

The scripture readings of Lent are full of imagery about turning away from sin, reforming our lives, admitting our faults, taking care of the poor and oppressed, and serving our brothers and sisters so that we may be transformed by having our hearts ready and open to follow Jesus completely.

The forty days of Lent are like being on a retreat—a time to look deeply at our lives and how we are doing on our journey to spiritual wholeness. For each weekday of Lent, the daily Mass readings are listed, followed by a short reflection and question for examination of your heart. Make some quiet time each morning and/or night to read, pray, write your thoughts down, and assess how you live out the scriptural call each day.

Ash Wednesday

• Joel 2:12–18 • 2 Corinthians 5:20–6:2
• Matthew 6:1–6; 16–18

Turn away from sin and be faithful to the Gospel!

Gather the people! Blow the trumpet and proclaim a fast! We begin our Lenten journey—a forty-day retreat for the whole church. Once again, we repent and call upon our loving God to help us grow stronger in our faith and to live it in love. God who is rich in mercy and slow to anger will purify and renew the hearts of all who ask it in prayer and who fast, do for others, and give to the poor.

 What will you do this Lent to make it a sacred time?

Thursday after Ash Wednesday

• Deuteronomy 30:15–20 • Luke 9:22–25
Blessed are they who hope in the Lord.

Choose life! Those who walk in the way of God are promised life. Jesus makes "the way" specific: to be disciples, we must deny ourselves and take up our own cross.

 How are the choices you are making today "choosing life"?

Friday after Ash Wednesday

• Isaiah 58:1–9a • Matthew 9:14–15

A heart contrite and humbled, O God, you will not spurn.

The fast God requires of us is a fast from indifference to the plight of others. We are to do what is just. Repeatedly, scripture spells out what makes for justice: to set free the oppressed, feed the hungry, release the imprisoned, shelter the homeless, and clothe the naked.

 How will you reach out to a person in need, support a just cause, contribute to a food bank or homeless shelter, or visit someone who is ill?

Saturday after Ash Wednesday

• Isaiah 58:9b–14 • Luke 5:27–32

Teach me your way, O Lord, that I may walk in your truth.

Follow me! What a simple command; an invitation by Jesus to be transformed. He came to heal the sick and change the hearts of sinners. As Jesus' disciples, we not only ask for his healing hand upon our hearts but must follow his example by caring for the weak and oppressed.

 What have you left behind to follow Jesus?

First Week of Lent

Monday

• Leviticus 19:1–2, 11–18 • Matthew 25:31–46

Your words, Lord, are spirit and life.

Love, love, love! How often we hear that in scripture. Who is the just person that will inherit the promised kingdom? Whoever puts into practice the commands of God, that is, whoever loves wholeheartedly, feeds the hungry, welcomes the stranger, clothes the naked, and visits the sick and imprisoned.

 Make time today to show love and care for another—by being kind, stopping to talk with a co-worker who seems stressed, inviting a neighbor or fellow parishioner for coffee, or sending a supportive email or text message.

Tuesday

• Isaiah 55:10–11 • Matthew 6:7–15

From all their distress, God rescues the just.

God knows what we need. The Our Father is a prayer of trust and confidence in God that what we need is heard. When we pray it, we ask forgiveness and express our willingness to forgive others, the true sign of a Christian.

 Spend time today praising and thanking God for all the good gifts you have received.

Wednesday

• Jonah 3:1–10 • Luke 11:29–32

A heart contrite and humbled, O God, you will not spurn.

At Jonah's warning, the people of Nineveh fasted and turned away from their sins and in response God spared them. So will God save us if we repent and reform our lives and believe in Jesus, Son of God, and our salvation.

 What needs reform in your life?

Thursday

• Esther C:12, 14–16, 23–25 • Matthew 7:7–12

Lord, on the day I called for help you answered.

When Queen Esther asked God for courage and persuasive words to save her people, God answered her prayer. God promises to hear our requests if we but ask and are faithful.

Pray today for what you need and for the needs of family and friends.

Friday

• Ezekiel 18:21–28 • Matthew 5:20–26

If you, O Lord, mark iniquities, who can stand?

The Lord rejoices whenever a person turns away from sin and from wishing harm on another. We are urged to always take the "high road" by thinking the best and making the first move toward forgiving or asking forgiveness. True repentance entails conforming to the spirit, not just the letter, of God's law.

 With whom do you need to be reconciled? How can you take the first step?

Saturday

• Deuteronomy 26:16–19 • Matthew 5:43–48

Blessed are they who follow the law of the Lord!

We are loved by God; we are sacred; we are God's own! God has made a covenant with us to keep us close if we follow the law, listen to his voice, and love—not just our neighbor, but even our enemy. Jesus explains that love of neighbor must supersede group loyalties, familial, and national ones. We must love even our enemies and pray for our persecutors.

 Today pray for or reach out to someone who has hurt you.

Second Week of Lent

Monday

• Daniel 9:4b–10 • Luke 6:36–38

Lord, do not deal with us according to our sins.

We often fail in our attempt to be faithful to God's law. But God is still faithful to us if we return wholeheartedly. In the Gospel, Jesus "kicks it up a notch." We are to be merciful, not judgmental, or we will be judged without mercy. If we give, we will be given gifts. We are to be generous in all things!

 What are gifts given to you by God? How do you share them with others?

Tuesday

• Isaiah 1:10, 16–20 • Matthew 23:1–12

To the upright I will show the saving power of God.

Wash yourselves clean! Change your ways and you will have the fullness of life, says our God. We not only have to learn to do good, but we must do good without hypocrisy or showiness. Jesus teaches by words and example that the greatest in the kingdom is the servant of all.

 How are you doing with your Lenten observances? What do you need to concentrate on?

Wednesday

• Jeremiah 18:18–20 • Matthew 20:17–28

Save me, O Lord, in your kindness.

As Jesus heads toward Jerusalem, where trial, condemnation, and death await him, the apostles quarrel about their status in the group. Jesus uses the occasion to explain the meaning of service. If you are to be great, you put yourself at the service of others. His suffering and death are the ultimate gifts of service to us.

 Today, take time to observe how you go out of your way to serve others—family, friends, co-workers, shopkeepers, store clerks.

Thursday

• Jeremiah 17:5–10 • Luke 16:19–31

Blessed are they who hope in the Lord.

The Lord probes our mind, tests our heart, and rewards our deeds. Nothing else matters with God, not our salaries, our status, our education, and our reputation. The lowliest beggar and the richest entrepreneur will both reap rewards if rooted in the Lord. God is our hope. It is God we trust.

 How have you trusted completely in God today?

Friday

• Genesis 37:3–4, 12–13a, 17b–28a • Matthew 21:33–34, 45–46

Remember the marvels the Lord has done.

Two violent stories. Joseph is sold into slavery by his jealous brothers, and Jesus' parable concerns a vineyard owner whose tenants murdered his servants, then his son. Both stories foreshadow the violence that will overtake Jesus, seen in the readings of Passion Sunday. The end point of both is redemption. Joseph redeems his dysfunctional family, while Jesus redeems the whole human family.

 Why was Jesus rejected by the chief priest and elders? Do you know someone who has been harmed while standing up for what is just? How can you express support for that person?

Saturday

• Micah 7:14–15, 18–20 • Luke 15:1-3, 11–32

The Lord is kind and merciful.

When his detractors whispered against him for welcoming sinners, Jesus told them the story of a reconciling father who welcomed back his returning son with joy, even after the boy had wasted his share of the family inheritance. It is such prodigals, not the "good," whom Jesus seeks to save. Our God is kind, merciful, and understanding.

 Reflect on a time when you took the easy way out. What happened? How did you grow from that experience?

Third Week of Lent

Monday

• 2 Kings 5:1–5ab • Luke 4:24–30

Athirst is my soul for the living God. When shall I go and behold the face of God?

Jesus enrages the synagogue in Nazareth by comparing himself with two prophets, Elisha and Elijah, both of whom worked miracles for people outside their tribal groups. No one who accepts God's Son will be left out of God's favor.

 Why were the people so enraged by Jesus?

Tuesday

• Daniel 3:25, 34–43 • Matthew 18:21-35

Remember your mercies, Lord.

What moves God is a humble and contrite spirit in a person. The compassion and mercy we want God to show us, we must extend to those around us as well. We must forgive always, not seven times but seventy-seven times—over and over again. Not an easy task.

 What do you do over and over that you find yourself asking forgiveness for? How can you change this pattern?

Wednesday

• Deuteronomy 4:1, 5–9 • Matthew 5:17–19

Praise the Lord, Jerusalem.

Through the commandments, God teaches us what we must do to become righteous. Jesus teaches that the commandments are fulfilled, not abolished, through him. Whoever is faithful and fulfills the commandments will enjoy a place of honor in the kingdom of God.

 Listen to God today. Jot down what you are hearing in prayer.

Thursday

• Jeremiah 7:23–28 • Luke 11:14–23

If today you hear God's voice, harden not your hearts.

Whatever lurks inside us causing us to disobey or refuse to hear the Lord is weak. God's strength is all we need if we are to repent and be faithful. Faith gives witness to the fact that the power of God is stronger than the power of evil. God wants us to be united with him, not set apart.

 When have you most noticed evil in the world?

Friday

• Hosea 14:2–10 • Mark 12:28–34

I am the Lord your God: hear my voice.

There are two great commandments: Love God with your whole heart, mind, and strength, and love your neighbor as yourself. How often we have heard that! If we practice this, we are not far from the heart of God. It takes love and great discipline!

 How do you practice observing these two commandments?

Saturday

• Hosea 6:1–6 • Luke 18:9–14

It is mercy I desire, not sacrifice.

What God desires from us is love—not lip service, praise, or mere dutiful action. Those who love God are fearless and humble enough to throw themselves completely on God's mercy.

 How have you put yourself completely in God's hands this Lent?

Fourth Week of Lent

Monday

• Isaiah 65:17–21 • John 4:43–54

I will praise you, Lord, for you have rescued me.

God is full of surprises! God promises, yet again, to create something new—new life, new ways of doing things, new relationships. We must be continually growing. Like the royal official who trusted Jesus to heal his son, we too can trust that God wants to heal us and delight in us. God is for us!

 Thank God today for newness in your life.

Tuesday

• Ezekiel 47:1–9,12   • John 5:1–16

The Lord of hosts is with us; our stronghold is the God of Jacob.

Jesus approached the sick man at the Bethesda pool and asked if he wanted to be healed. He wanted to make the man whole. His command is to "sin no more," be free, be happy, delight in the Lord, do good works, live a godly life. Lent does not have to be somber, but a time in which we learn how close God wants to be to each of us.

 How do you delight in God today? Spend some time in quiet prayer.

Wednesday

• Isaiah 49:8–15   • John 5:17–30

The Lord is gracious and merciful.

God loves us as tenderly as the parents of a newborn. In Isaiah, God is likened to a mother who would never forsake her infant or fail to lavish tenderness on the child. All that God does is to ensure that we have a relationship with him that is everlasting. In John's Gospel, Jesus speaks of God as his Father who loves the Son eternally, the one who sent him, the one whose will he seeks to do. They are ever linked as we are with God.

 Pray for your mother, father, grandmother, and grandfather today. Reflect on their love that has sustained you.

Thursday

• Exodus 32:7–14   • John 5:31–47

Remember us, O Lord, as you favor your people.

Most likely we have never seen God's form or heard God's voice. But if we believe that Jesus is the Son of God, we can see what the Father is like through him. The Father has sent Jesus so that we might understand and believe more deeply. Yet, sadly, even in Jesus' time, many did not. Lent gives us this time to probe more deeply into who God is for us.

 Make time today to read and pray this Gospel passage. What jumps off the page for you?

Friday

• Wisdom 2:1a, 12–22   • John 7:1–2, 10, 25–30

The Lord is close to the brokenhearted.

Toward the end of his life on earth, Jesus was something of a fugitive, a wanted man. In the Gospel reading for today, the crowds are getting restless and Jesus tries to make them understand that he is from the Father. They tried to arrest him but they were afraid. Yet when the time was right, Jesus fulfilled his life's mission, faced his enemies, forgave his persecutors, and offered his life for the world. These events are foreshadowed in the first reading from Wisdom.

 What was the mission of Jesus? How did he fulfill it?

Saturday

• Jeremiah 11:18–20 • John 7:40–53

O Lord, my God, in you I take refuge.

The passage from Jeremiah increases the tension—plots are being hatched, people are looking to destroy the innocent, the trusting lamb is being led to the slaughter. In the Gospel, the crowd is confused and trying to understand Jesus as a prophet, his lineage, and where the Christ (Messiah) is to come from. Is he the Messiah or not?

 What do you say to those who wonder about who Christ is?

Fifth Week of Lent

Monday

• Daniel 13:1–9, 15–17, 19–30, 33–62
• John 8:1–11 or John 8:12–20

O Lord, when your glory appears, my joy will be full.

Susanna was falsely accused of adultery. A woman was brought before Jesus who was caught in the act of adultery. Jesus refuses to judge the woman, but rather asks her to go and sin no more. The scribes and Pharisees were once again trying to trick Jesus. He showed that he chose mercy over condemnation.

 As you interact with people today, show mercy rather than judgment.

Tuesday

- Numbers 21:4–9 • John 8:21–30

O Lord, hear my prayer, and let my cry come to you.

When Moses lifted up a bronze serpent on a pole, God saved those who looked on it from a venomous death. In John's Gospel, Jesus alludes to that story in explaining his own impending death on a cross: "When you lift up the Son of Man, you will come to realize that I AM."

 How does reflecting on the passion and death of Christ heal you?

Wednesday

- Daniel 3:14–20, 91–92, 95 • John 8:31–42

Glory and praise forever!

Three young men, Shadrach, Meshach, and Abednego, are put into a white-hot furnace because they would not renounce their faith. They are saved when one like the "son of God" appears with them in the flames. The king believes and sets them free. In the Gospel, Jesus wrestles with the Pharisees over his identity and authority. If you choose to be a disciple, the truth will set you free.

 Have you made a commitment to be a disciple of Jesus? If so, what made that happen?

Thursday

• Genesis 17:3–9 • John 8:51–59

The Lord remembers his covenant forever.

God's promise to make an everlasting pact with Abraham's descendants has been fulfilled. In turn, Jesus promises everlasting life to all who are true to his word. John shows Jesus confounding his hearers with a declaration of his oneness with God, "before Abraham came to be, I AM."

 How do you renew your covenant with God each day?

Friday

• Jeremiah 20:10–13 • John 10:31–42

In my distress I called upon the Lord, and he heard my voice.

They picked up rocks to stone Jesus. Some thought that Jesus was blaspheming by equating himself with the Father, yet Jesus claimed to be God's Son. He performed the works of God—who else could do that? They did not believe him.

 How do you, as Jesus' disciple, perform the works of God? What more could you do?

Saturday

• Ezekiel 37:21–28 • John 11:45–56

The Lord will guard us as a shepherd guards his flock.

In Ezekiel, the Lord speaks of there being one shepherd, one prince, with all God's people, living together in a covenant of peace. In the passage from John, the high priest fears that all will believe in Jesus and the Romans will punish them. The plot to kill him was hatched.

 How does the Lord shepherd you each day? Do you allow this willingly or resist?

Holy Week

Monday of Holy Week

• Isaiah 42:1–7 • John 12:1–11

The Lord is my light and my salvation.

The suffering servant is upheld by God. He works to establish justice and free people from darkness and confinement—things that hold us back from knowing God fully. The suffering servant foreshadows the Messiah—grasped by the hand of God and set as a light to the nations. In the Gospel, Mary, grateful for Jesus raising her brother Lazarus from the dead, anoints the feet of Jesus with costly perfume. This act foreshadows his death and anointing for burial. The time was getting nearer.

 What will you do to make this week a special time of prayer and reflection?

Tuesday of Holy Week

• Isaiah 49:1–6 • John 13:21–33, 36–38

I will sing of your salvation.

Jesus was troubled at table. He announced that one of his chosen would betray him. The reaction of the disciples was disbelief. No one could imagine this. And yet it was true.

 What would your reaction have been if you were at the table with Jesus?

Wednesday of Holy Week

• Isaiah 50:4–9a • Matthew 26:14–25

Lord, in your great love, answer me.

God opens our senses to hear and proclaim the goodness and power of God. God helps those who are faithful, yet demands sacrifice. Jesus begins the last days of his earthly ministry and is betrayed by one he trusts. How can this be? The disciples do not understand what he is saying and cannot imagine it. Yet one among them has started the betrayal.

 What speaks to you in these two scripture passages?

The Easter Triduum

Holy Thursday

• Exodus 12:1–8, 11–14 • 1 Corinthians 11:23–26
• John 13:1–15

Our blessing cup is a communion with the blood of Christ.

Jesus demonstrates what true love and leadership is—washing the feet of those you serve. He shows that this is the way they are to take his message into the world. Not by lording it over others but in true humility and loving service. Christ is the model.

Spend some time in silence with the Lord this evening after the Holy Thursday Mass of the Lord's Supper. Keep the Paschal Fast, which stretches from the Holy Thursday Mass through the Easter Vigil on Holy Saturday. Eat sparingly, refrain from music, television, or other extras in your life. This is a fast of anticipation, helping us mark the sacredness of these days.

Good Friday

• Isaiah 52:13–53:12 • Hebrews 4:14–16; 5:7–9
• John 18:1–19:42

Father, I put my life in your hands.

This day is about innocent suffering. Nothing has been done by Jesus to warrant suffering and death and yet it happens. Jesus carries his cross, has people assist him, weep for him, and call out to him—and yet he is alone. In our lives we have all experienced these dark moments: catastrophic illness, the loss of a loved one, betrayal, loneliness, depression. We join our suffering to the suffering of Jesus. We believe that the darkness of suffering gives way to the light of new life in Christ.

 Make this day special by spending quiet time with the Lord in prayer and by attending the Celebration of the Lord's Passion or the Stations of the Cross in your parish. This is a day we abstain from meat and fast. Eat sparingly and let your hunger lead you to pray for those in need this day.

Holy Saturday, the Easter Vigil

Old Testament Readings:

• Genesis: 1:1–2:2 • Genesis 22:1–18 • Exodus 14:15–15:1
• Isaiah 54:5–14 • Isaiah 55:1–11 • Baruch 3:9–15, 32–4:4
• Ezekiel 36:16–17a, 18–28

Epistle:

Romans 6:3–11

Gospel:

Luke 24:1–12

Alleluia, alleluia, alleluia!

The Easter Vigil is the highpoint of the entire liturgical year. That is why the Church provides nine readings for this holy night. Some parishes will use them all, others only use the minimum required, which are three from the Old Testament, the epistle from Paul, and the Gospel reading. All are cited above for your use.

We break the darkness of this holy night with the light of Christ that shines from the new fire, then the Easter Candle, and finally individual candles as we process into a darkened church. The readings that proclaim God's saving power are joyously proclaimed. New Christians are brought to life in the sacraments of initiation—baptism, confirmation, and eucharist. Together we feast at the table of the Lord as we recognize his presence in the breaking of the bread, the sharing of the cup of salvation, and the joyous power of the resurrection.

Celebrate all that you have reflected on this Lent and Holy Week by participating in the Easter Vigil at your parish. Let go of what is dead in you and make ready for new life. Courageously and full of hope, open your heart!

Easter Sunday

• Acts of the Apostles 10:34a, 37–43 • Colossians 3:1–4
• John 20:1–9

This is the day that the Lord has made; let us rejoice and be glad.

Mary Magdalene is the first to arrive at the tomb that Easter morning. She sees something has happened, the stone has been moved. She runs to tell Peter. When Peter and the other disciples arrive they discover the empty tomb and discarded burial cloths. Truly something has happened! The Lord has been raised! Alleluia!

 What has happened in your life because of this past Lent and this Easter celebration?

Facilitator's Weekly Evaluation Form

Also available for download at www.avemariapress.com

Lenten Reflection Groups

Date _____

Facilitator _____

Phone _____ Email _____

1. Session: One   Two   Three   Four   Five   Six
   (circle the appropriate week)

   Number in group _____

   Number in attendance _____

   Place of meeting _____

2. In general, the meeting was:

   Excellent   Good   Fair   Poor *(circle one)*

3. What worked well?

4. What we might improve:

5. Are there any questions or problems
   that need further attention?

6. How are members responding to the reflection material?

7. Are members participating in an Action? If so, describe it.

8. Responses to the parish questions: *(write in the
   questions as well as the members' ideas)*

Next Meeting:

Date _____ Time _____

Place _____